Before You Depart

God's Touch before Eternity

Nanette M. Holloway, MS, RN

BEFORE YOU DEPART

Copyright © 2020 Oklahoma Rose Publishing

All Rights Reserved

Imprint: Independently Published

No part of this publication may be reproduced, stored in a retrieval system, or transmitted in any form or by any means — electronic, mechanical, photocopy, recording, or any other — except for brief quotations in printed reviews, without the prior permission of the author.

Throughout this publication, scripture passages are referenced with the following copyrights: New International Version ©1985 The Zondervan Corporation, King James Version Public Domain, New American Standard Bible ©1960 The Lockman Foundation, The Amplified Bible ©1965 The Lockman Foundation. The American Standard Version and the King James Version are available in the public domain.

Printed in the United States of America

BEFORE YOU DEPART

"This poignantly written work communicates to the reader the real, raw, and ever-present emotions and love that accompany deep, acute and finally chronic grief following the physical loss of a cherished loved one, in this case a parent. Written in the first person, the author expresses all of the many feelings and personal perceptions of the experiences that have accompanied this father/daughter' life long journey together including her father's life-threatening diagnosis, terminal illness and death. The day to day struggles of providing holistic care for a loved one as well as juggling all of the roles required in daily family life with a husband and a growing family are also addressed in vivid, unvarnished dialog. Woven throughout this heart wrenching journey the author addresses difficult, longstanding, unresolved and heartbreaking personal interactions with family members that are realities in most families, providing us with a testimony that only prayer, unselfishness, respect for others and forgiveness are the key to manageable resolution and restoration of love within strained and estranged long-standing family relationships that further complicate and estrange families during and after the loss of love one. In addition, the recollections of the end of her father's life and managing to spend as much quality time with him as possible and verbally expressing her feelings of love, not knowing if each time spent together might be or would be the last interaction together on this earth, prompts deep soul searching and grief work for everyone that has lost a cherished love one. The long and painful process of grief work including anger, guilt and remorse as each individual seeks to find meaning and resolution with the memories, loss of the relationship, and making sense of it all so one can go on with life is also addressed in vivid, personal detail. And last but not least, light is fully shed on gaps and multiple opportunities for improvement in the healthcare system as grief counselors and grief services commonly provided to the bereaved are clearly addressed. Glaring in these short comings are truths that most individuals involved in proving much needed essential grief services mean well; but lack the intimate

BEFORE YOU DEPART

knowledge of grief and grieving and do not have a clue "what the bereaved are feeling". Thank you Nanette for making this real and letting each of us know by example that the process of grief work is painful, but essential to make sense of it all and find meaning in the acute and chronic phases of this process so we do not get stuck here and so our lives can go on with dignity, peace, and spiritual purpose."

-Barbara Hannah, EdD, MS, BS, RN

"Nanette Holloway has beautifully recreated her journey through the illness and death of her father. She writes with passion and empathy, describing her feelings of grief, anger, fatigue, and in the end, renewed faith in the God who loves us. Through her journey Nanette comes to recognize that the struggle is both physical and spiritual. I believe other caregivers will find an engaging realism in Nanette's self-reflection along a path that leads to healing."

-Dr. Ray Crawford

BEFORE YOU DEPART

DEDICATIONS

This book is dedicated to my dad, Carl W. Martin who taught me tenacity and strength and loved my brother and me with all his heart.

My mom, Edna Martin, who nurtured my creativity and faith in Christ.

To CJay Martin, my brother and friend who shared in this journey.

BEFORE YOU DEPART

BEFORE YOU DEPART

TABLE OF CONTENTS

CHAPTER 1 11
CHAPTER 2 17
CHAPTER 3 21
CHAPTER 4 25
CHAPTER 5 31
CHAPTER 6 37
CHAPTER 7 43
CHAPTER 8 49
CHAPTER 9 55
CHAPTER 10 61
CHAPTER 11 67
CHAPTER 12 73
INVITATION 81

BEFORE YOU DEPART

Before You Depart

God's Touch before Eternity

BEFORE YOU DEPART

BEFORE YOU DEPART

CHAPTER 1

Although Carl Martin's death was difficult, life began in an idyllic small-town farming community. A simpler time with simple hope of survival a better future ahead.

The small white farmhouse perched on a hill overlooked a farmland tapestry as far as the eye could see. Two miles from the small town, situated in the northeast corner of Oklahoma.

Bright sunshine filtered through the lace curtains covering ample windows. The simplicity of functional furniture graced the living room, welcoming all who entered.

Nan Martin gave birth to Carl on September 4, 1910. He was number three out of five boys raised by Len and Nan.

The family was poor but self-sufficient. Nan, like others in her day, grew vegetables and canned provisions for the winter. She raised chickens and sold eggs and butter in town. Livestock raised on the farm provided meat. Corn was a staple. Other crops grown in the area included sorghum cane and wheat.

Nan provided hearty farmhouse meals for her five hungry boys. The smell of freshly baked bread filled the quaint home. Accolades of her good cooking brought rave reviews long after her death.

During Carl's high school years, Nan worked in the field alongside Len so her boys could graduate from high school and earn a diploma.

BEFORE YOU DEPART

The trip to the one-room schoolhouse was two miles on horseback. No such thing as a snow day in the early 1900's.

Carl told stories of helping the neighbor harvest and clarify sorghum cane. A team of mules were used to mill the cane, and the juice boiled down into sweet syrup better known as sorghum. The reward for his labor was a gallon of the refined brown syrup ready to compliment cornbread.

Growing up during the Depression created a strong work ethic in Carl. As a young man he followed the crops harvesting whatever was available, eventually arriving in Southern California. He married at age 40. He and his wife, Edna moved to Littlerock, California.

Carl became a father for the first time at the age of 48. My brother was born, followed by my own birth, 19 months later. Mom was twelve years younger than Carl who adored and loved both his children. He worked at Lockheed Aircraft in Palmdale for 33 years.

The town of Littlerock was renowned for peaches and pears, an orchard oasis in the middle of the Mohave Desert. Orchards were everywhere. Pink and white blossoms provided a nonstop parade of color in spring. Followed by a harvest of fat juicy peaches and succulent pears in summer. Fruit stands dotted Pearblossom Highway where growers sold the prized fruit. The crops drew people from as far as Los Angeles and the surrounding area. Some growers shipped their crops to market.

Carl cultivated his own small orchard — five acres of peaches and pears.

I graduated from Palmdale High School, then ventured to Tulsa, Oklahoma. Drawn to Dad's roots in Oklahoma, I graduated from Oral Roberts University with a degree in nursing and married my husband, Andy.

I always enjoyed visits to Dad's family farm and the climate which differed from the California desert.

Andy and I had two boys, Marty and Mitch, three years apart. We started married life in Tulsa, but we both desired acreage in the country. Ten years later the opportunity presented itself, and we began life on our eighty-acre farm.

Andy owned and drove a semi-truck and tanker that delivered gasoline. He was a hard worker, driving nights so he could spend more time with the boys and me. He made fun out of work on the farm and provided endless laughter and

BEFORE YOU DEPART

entertainment for the boys. He wrestled and played football in high school, so he retained a muscular physique.

Carl was 86 when he moved to our farm. Mom had died ten years previous. As Dad advanced in age I worried about him living in California with no family close by. He first moved back to his hometown in Welch and lived near his one living brother.

His mind was still clear and sharp. Arthritic hips slowed his pace, otherwise he was fortunate to have good health. His favorite pastime was reading, followed by television watching with the set turned up to blaring decibels, audible to his age-deafened ears. He ventured out daily for lunch, finding all the best eateries in a thirty-mile radius.

Like Ferdinand the Bull, Dad was known for his strong, stubborn will. When his mind was set, there was no changing it. The only right way was Carl's way. Everyone in the family knew this truth and accepted it. His voice had a thunderous bite, alerting listeners to attention. Yet his carefully constructed veneer on the outside protected his soft heart from outside threats. A man of few words, he was always direct and straight-forward.

The bull was on the move when he was ready to move onto the farm. He thundered on the phone, "Dolly, I have a builder coming to give an estimate for the apartment. He'll be there tomorrow about noon."

We had talked briefly about building an apartment. The subject had not come up again until now, approximately four months later. I thought *I don't know if I'm ready for this*, but replied, "Okay." Apprehension welled up in my throat as I hung up the phone.

I worked with distraction, straightening the house, anxious to talk to Andy.

Seeming like an eternity, Andy finally woke up. He immediately sensed tension and asked, "What's wrong?"

With a hesitant pause, I said, "Dad's sending a builder tomorrow for his apartment."

"Oh, okay. We'll see what he comes up with."

Relieved and reassured from Andy's reaction, I started dinner.

Ready or not the builder came, and the apartment was built.

The time came for Dad to move in. I took the following week off work to help him.

BEFORE YOU DEPART

Not willing to wait, he moved himself the next day. His car was stuffed with personal items haphazardly thrown in. The apartment was christened as countertops were strewn with tools of all types, dishes, silverware, pots and pans. He pushed himself to the limit, then simply stopped for a nap. With Dad, we never knew what might happen next. The countertop items eventually found their places, later rather than sooner.

One thing was for certain, Dad was faithful to family. He rarely called me by my given name, Nanette, but used the endearment of Dolly. At birth, I weighed three pounds and three ounces, essentially a delicate doll. The name stuck.

The adjustment to his habitation next door was smooth. Dad usually came over for dinner but went out to eat for lunch. Our sons, Marty and Mitch went to see him regularly, enjoying Cartoon Network. Dad rented a satellite dish for his television.

Dad lived next door for approximately five years. We planned family days and went out to eat with him on Saturdays when Andy was free.

Andy enjoyed my dad and helped him whenever he could. One day Dad's hearing aids quit working. Andy offered to take him into Tulsa to have the hearing aids serviced. Andy napped in the car.

Dad came out of the store, climbed in the passenger seat and said, "They want to talk to you."

Tired from working the night before, Andy trudged in.

The clerk behind the desk wore fear on his face. With the phone in his hand, he said, "Please sir, I don't want any trouble."

When Andy returned to the car, he asked Dad, "What did you say to him? Are you trying to get me in trouble?"

With an ornery grin, Dad sheepishly looked out the passenger window and chuckled. "I told him that you were going to get things straight with these hearing aids one way or another."

Laughing, Andy replied, "I can't let you threaten those poor people. I'm going in next time."

They decided to try a different hearing aid place. To avoid any conflict Andy escorted Dad into the store. Hearing aids were essential before returning home. The requisite errand was accomplished.

BEFORE YOU DEPART

Dad began to have difficulty swallowing his food. One evening he came to the house and complained, "Dolly, I have something stuck in my throat." Our two boys were already in bed, and Andy had left for work.

Desperate, I called Andy, "Dad needs to go to the emergency room." Although he was almost to work, after a fifty-mile drive, he turned around and drove Dad to the emergency room in a neighboring town thirty miles away.

The doctor informed Andy that he would have to take Dad to a larger hospital, ninety miles away. They made the trip.

In the larger hospital, they had the equipment to remove a piece of meat and stretch Dad's esophagus. This problem happened on more than one occasion. Then the doctor began to routinely stretch Dad's esophagus.

The gastroenterologist wanted a biopsy of Dad's esophagus. "Your father will need to be sedated, so someone will have to accompany him and drive him home."

The appointment was made, and the biopsy completed the following week. Doctor Eden entered the waiting room and led me to his office. "I'm pretty sure your dad has cancer of the esophagus. We won't know for sure until we have the biopsy results, but the tissue looks cancerous."

Tears welled up in my eyes and I asked, "What kind of treatment options are available?" We were embarking on an unknown journey with phantasmal shadows lurking on all sides. My head was filled with magnified fear, dread and apprehension.

"We will discuss that next week. We can tell your father the diagnosis together. In the meantime, go home and enjoy your dad."

BEFORE YOU DEPART

CHAPTER 2

The following week arrived too soon. Dad and I waited in the exam room. He knew nothing of what the doctor had told me. I hoped the doctor was wrong.

But hope was dashed as Doctor Eden announced, "I have some bad news. The laboratory results of the biopsy were positive for a slow-growing cancer."

Doctor Eden paused. An eternity passed while the news hit us, comprehension denied. Dad nodded with tears in his eyes, ready for the doctor to continue.

"Food catches in your throat because as the cancer grows, the opening of your esophagus is slowly closing."

"How long do I have, Doc?"

"One month to one year. You've probably had this cancer for a long time. You have some different options. We can surgically remove the cancer in the esophagus and place a synthetic tube inside.

"Another option is radiation therapy entailing several trips to the hospital in Tulsa. Or a tube can be placed into the stomach and you would then have tube feedings, no longer eating food. The final option is to place a mesh tube into the esophagus. The mesh tube will keep the esophagus open, allowing food to enter the stomach. Eventually the cancer will grow around the mesh openings and cause difficulty swallowing once again.

"I've made a list with your options. You can think about them over the next week. All treatments will be done in the Tulsa hospital. You can call the office with your decision and we'll make arrangements for your choice at that time."

The drive home was somber. Dad said, "Let's get a shake." He chose his usual chocolate shake while I wanted a chocolate vanilla twist cone. We assimilated the information over our frosty snacks.

Dad asked, "Did you know?"

"Yes, he told me last week."

Fear and doubt flooded my weary mind. *How was Dad dealing with this news? Which treatment should he choose? Would homeschooling still be an option? Would there be time to take care of my dad and teach the boys as well? Should the boys witness his decline? What if Dad gets too sick and needs round-the-clock care?*

Sleep was intermittent that night, mingled with worry and dread. Tossing and turning, I moved to the couch, hoping for a geographical fix for my troublesome thoughts. My stomach was tight and my head ached. All the "what if" possibilities flooded my mind.

The next morning was Saturday, and Andy had the day off. We sat down for coffee and breakfast. Sensing my anxious state of shock, disbelief and uncertainty, Andy said, "Why don't you go have a quiet time?"

With reluctance, I grabbed my Bible. I had plenty of arguments for God but brought the heavy burden before him. Tears of desperation launched my prayer, and I cried for the first time since the nightmare began.

The journey ahead is impossible. The pain of watching my dad decline and suffer the way my mom did will be too much for me. How can I possibly take care of my boys and my dad at the same time? I'm not ready to lose Dad. This cannot be happening. Dad has always been so healthy. I don't want to be a nurse and caregiver. I just want to be Dad's daughter. He needs to continue to be okay so he can continue to be my dad.

I poured out my distraught heart to God and turned to Matthew 7:7-11 in the Amplified version.

"Ask and keep on asking and it will be given to you; seek and keep on seeking and you will find; knock and keep on knocking and the door will be opened to you. For everyone who keeps on asking receives, and he who keeps on seeking finds, and to him who keeps on knocking, it will be opened. Or what man is there among you who, if his son asks for bread, will give him a stone? Or if he asks for a fish, will give him a snake? If you then, evil as you are, know how to give good and advantageous gifts to your children, how much more will your Father who is in heaven give what is good and advantageous to those who keep on asking Him?"

On bowed knees my mounting requests for the impossible cascaded from a pool of worry to prayerful possibility. The list was long. The most desperate need was a reconciliation with Dad, who always seemed angry. If dinner was ready at six o'clock, he wanted it at five o'clock.

The relationship of daughter and father had shifted from doting to resentment on his part. Now he barked impossible requests, needing something beyond anyone's ability to render. The standard of approval was impossible to reach.

My presumptuous request was that family curses be broken, including toxic shame, guilt, depression and victimization. The curses overshadowed life in a myriad of horrendous manifestations.

The next request was salvation for my cousin Emma. She was three years older than me, but we were still friends. She had been a Christian as a young teen, but she had become bitter over the years and lost her faith. She became belligerent with any mention of God or religion. Emma was a free spirit with no particular direction or moral compass. She liked beer and married men. Our relationship deteriorated as she ventured through her reckless path, common values dwindling.

BEFORE YOU DEPART

Since her own father died years earlier, Emma had an endearing attachment to Dad. He often welcomed her, gave her money, and took her out to eat at one of his favorite diners.

Emma inserted herself into our lives every six to eight months when the drama of life threatened sanity. She vented about her self-created chaos, only to return to the same unacceptable situation. Her monumental problems only God could fix.

Through tears of grief, I clamored on in petition. My hope was that God would hear and answer my presumptuous pleas.

Finally there were no more tears. My mind quieted in relief. I closed my eyes to savor the moment. A peaceful sigh released the tension carried between my shoulder blades.

But there was more. Through the quiet I felt a distinct inaudible whisper from God into my heart.

"Are you willing to care for your dad in his final journey? The season will be short."

My heart filled with awe, relief, reverence and praise. My prayer had been heard. Humbly I replied, "Yes, Lord."

Rising up in abject surrender to God's will, I seized the provision of renewed spiritual strength and hope for whatever we would face.

BEFORE YOU DEPART

CHAPTER 3

The next morning the boys and I made our way across the yard to Dad's apartment. Entering the room, the usual aroma of Bengay accosted us. The cream a necessary ointment for Dad's arthritic joints.

We had already been up early for school. The boys watched cartoons while Dad and I shared a pot of coffee.

Dad loudly stirred his coffee, adding cream and sugar while hitting the sides of the cup with the teaspoon. The habit woke me as a child and irritated my mom. Dad's muffled hearing didn't hear the clang and clatter. He announced, "I'm going to have that mesh put in. What exactly does that mesh do?"

I handed Dad the picture of what the stent looked like along with a brief explanation the doctor had given me. The stent looked like a metal mesh tube, the same size as the esophagus which extended from the back of the throat to the stomach. The stent would be placed where the cancer grew and blocked food particles. It was strong enough to gently hold the esophagus open so food could pass into the stomach. The procedure was palliative, focused on relief of symptoms, but not curative like chemotherapy.

I accepted Dad's decision and made the arrangements for the procedure.

The next week I took Dad to Tulsa for the procedure. The appointment set for seven am, with arrival time at six. That meant we had to start at five am.

Dad was extra quiet with a frightened look in his normally twinkling eyes. He took medicine to empty his bowel the evening before and had nothing to eat or

BEFORE YOU DEPART

drink since 4:00 pm yesterday. As we got in the car for our hour journey, he said, "I didn't sleep a wink last night, Dolly."

"Here, take this medicine. The doctor gave you this to take before the procedure. It will settle your nerves."

"Okay, Dolly. I guess we'd better go." I noted a tone of apprehension.

"I sure do love you, Dad."

"I love you the mostest, Dolly."

The starlit night seemed to welcome us down the long curving driveway, the section line road and finally to the turnpike. The quiet darkness interrupted by an occasional headlight from opposing traffic. Dad slept most of the way. Waking occasionally, he quietly looked out the window. He seemed to be withdrawn, not making eye contact. The city lights in Tulsa beamed the way to the hospital entrance.

The procedure was completed without incident. We were headed home by eight o'clock. Dad, still sedated from the procedure, slept most of the way.

Certain precautions were necessary. The valve going to the stomach was now held open with the stent. Food could travel back up the esophagus and cause Dad to vomit or to aspirate food into his lungs and cause pneumonia.

Several changes were made to prevent aspiration. The head of his bed needed to be elevated with bricks. He had to learn to eat smaller frequent meals. Dad needed to sit up for thirty minutes after eating, and he could not eat for two hours prior to bedtime.

The doctor also instructed us to keep several clean towels available in case he began to hemorrhage from the cancerous tumor and vomited blood. Should that occur, he would probably bleed to death.

As we adjusted to the new norm, Andy helped me put bricks under Dad's bed.

Three days later, Dad barked, "I can't sleep with those bricks under the bed. You're going to have to take them out."

Obediently, with the boys' help, I accommodated his defiant request. *Didn't Dad know he could aspirate and die from pneumonia? The doctor had instructed him to adjust his bed. He needed to be compliant if he wanted this process to work. What would the doctor say about Dad's stubbornness?*

The following week, I took Dad back to the doctor.

Doctor Eden asked, "How are things going?"

BEFORE YOU DEPART

Exasperated, I spoke up, "He won't put the bricks under his bed."

"Don't be alarmed. We're working for your dad. As long as he is doing some of the other things he needs to do, then we have to accept that he may not do everything. He's the boss and he's going to choose the recommendations he can live with as well as those he will not accept."

He continued to commend my dad on what he was doing right.

Reassured, I nodded. I could let go of needing him to be the perfect patient. I did not have to be the nurse who made sure he was compliant. The different perspective presented by the doctor brought relief from futile attempts to control Dad's poor choices. I was free to be his daughter rather than the demanding caregiver.

Although our morning rituals remained unaltered, one significant change occurred. During my quiet times with God, His presence met me in a new way. I had never been a morning person. Now I woke up early, as if God was urging me to enter into His presence through reading my Bible and saying my prayers.

God infused my devotions, thrilling my heart for an hour. Almost tangible waves of warmth and peace washed over me. All cares and worries ceased to matter. The Holy Spirit gave me a new joy, which is one of the gifts of the Spirit mentioned in Galatians 5:22 NIV, *"But the fruit of the Holy Spirit, (The work which His Presence within accomplishes), is love, joy, peace, patience, kindness, faithfulness gentleness, self-control. Against such there is no law."*

Nehemiah 8:10 reminded me, *"Do not grieve, for the joy of the Lord is your strength."* Joy is a spiritual state of happiness and well-being, independent of surrounding circumstances.

The joy God gave me was a deep happiness inside my heart and soul that no one could take. The emotion was new for me. I had struggled with depression most of my adult life. This joy was like a protection for my heart and emotions that overpowered the threat of depression. In the mornings I was filled with valiant purpose. God offered me His joy for the day ahead. I eagerly received His divine provision.

But by the end of the day I was exhausted. All strength and joy depleted. The schooling of the boys and caregiving for my dad consumed the long days.

The Lord was teaching me to abide with Him more closely. Some days my focus on God was quickly distracted by the problem of the day. Dad needed immediate

BEFORE YOU DEPART

attention. For instance, calling the pharmacy to reorder medications or filling his medication planner.

New and different challenges presented themselves. Each day was conquered, assisted by God silently equipping me through the struggle.

One day Dad came home with tears in his eyes. He threw a folder on the table.

"I'm gonna' die. I just made all my funeral arrangements. Everything is in the folder." Without waiting for a reply, he retreated to the bedroom.

The reality of pending death was no longer a tacit possibility. Reality diffused denial for a brief moment. But there was still no time or date.

I didn't see my dad until later that evening when I brought him dinner. We sat in silence. Fighting the fear of rejection, I crossed the room and gave him a hug. "I love you. I'm sorry."

"I love you the mostest."

"No, I love you the mostest."

We smiled through moist eyes.

He finished his dinner, then promptly threw up.

BEFORE YOU DEPART

CHAPTER 4

Dad chuckled as he opened his huge, oversized Valentine's Day cards. One from Andy and I and one from Marty and Mitch. I also made heart-shaped sugar cookies which he and the boys liked.

I was always searching for ways to let Dad know how much he was loved, trying to bridge the tensions which had developed in our relationship. Looking back, I wonder if he had been resentful over moving close to us, a constant reminder of his crumbling independence. I was passive and easy to blame.

Another issue contributing to resentment may have been role reversal. The child taking control of an aging parent with the occasional two-year-old mentality. Taking over became more and more necessary. Setting boundaries with an offended Ferdinand was not easy. A resistant throw of a lethal horn was always meant to keep me in my place.

Dealing with conflict generally sent me into emotional retreat. When the bull was unhappy, or anyone else for that matter, I felt the tensions rise. I had a sixth sense indicating unhappiness, keen to the slightest ripple in electromagnetic energy. Then came the tilt mode if the energy inched toward anger.

BEFORE YOU DEPART

The sixth sense was my warning to take flight on the emotional roller coaster that would remove me from the real or imagined danger. The roller coaster took me higher and faster, spinning me into emotional panic. My throat tightened, matched by a racing heartbeat and shallow, rapid respirations.

The only relief from the extreme emotions boiled over into heated tears. Crying was the only safe thing to do, or so it seemed. I could cry until the emotions played out. The tears insured temporary, counterfeit relief.

For the time being, the cookies and cards were tamping tempers in preparation for a good day. Physically, Dad seemed to be doing well. He was up and around, joining in the joyful mood of Saint Valentine's Day.

"How are you today, Dad?"

"Oh about the same, Dolly." The answer never changed, for a really good day or a really bad day. The answer was a joke between Andy and me since we already knew the answer.

As we finished dunking Valentine cookies in coffee, the boys asked if they could invite a friend to spend the night. We had completed school for the day, and since it was Friday, I agreed. They needed to have fun with friends. I could let them play outside while I worried about Dad's next need and the ever present threat of death—my compulsion to defy the beast.

Arrangements made, their friend came over and the boys ran down to the creek to play, with plenty of cookies when they needed a break from the cold temperatures. They were laughing in their own world, which made me grateful they were occupied.

That evening the boys settled down to watch a movie. Dad pulled into the driveway, honking frantically. He was visibly short of breath. Gasping with panic, he was able to say, "I need to go to the ER, Dolly."

As adrenaline pumped, I switched gears. I gave the boys instructions not to break anything and to call Andy at work. "Let him know what happened and call your friend's mother." I grabbed my coat and purse and jumped into the driver's seat.

BEFORE YOU DEPART

We were forty minutes away from the emergency room. Calling an ambulance was pointless since our back roads were not marked. The ambulance was twenty minutes away, but only if they could find us.

Driving faster than usual, I prayed *God, please help us make it in time.* I did not want to do CPR on my dad. I attempted to hide my own fear, tormented by sinister outcomes. All I could do was drive. I had to focus on driving.

"Slow down, Dolly. The bumpy roads are hard on me." Reluctantly I slowed down, thankful his tone was gentle. His eyes showed a terror I had never seen before.

"I sure do love you, Dolly." The endearment melted my heart and my guard came down, grateful for the reminder of his love.

Gripping the steering wheel as if to will us to the ER, I replied, "I love you the mostest." Tears welled up in my eyes. I was eager for the affection and deep feeling of connectedness between us, hoping endearments would continue.

"I'm sorry you had to leave the boys. I know all this is hard on you."

"I think they'll be okay. I'm glad to do it." I couldn't think about the boys. I had to keep my focus on the road ahead. One worry at a time was more than enough.

Dad kept telling me how much he loved me, which made me worry all the more that we might not make it in time. *Did he have a premonition, and needed to leave on good terms?* The mixed emotions of near-death panic and gratitude for a long-lost relationship seemed to urge us to our desired destination.

Finally we arrived. The nurse began working. First she put oxygen on Dad, followed by taking a set of vital signs. She was the only nurse in the small ER which had other patients as well. After an hour of waiting on blood work and chest x-ray results, they informed us Dad would be admitted. Thankful we had made it on time, I breathed prayers of thanksgiving.

BEFORE YOU DEPART

Dad reached for my hand while the nurse worked. He contentedly patted my hand like he did when I was a little girl. A peacefulness settled between us. I didn't want the moment to end. Occasionally he would playfully squeeze my hand a little too hard, and I played back with a hard squeeze. My heart was thrilled and full of gratitude for the familiar affections of long ago, overflowing with a love for my dad I thought had been lost.

Well after midnight, I blew Dad a kiss and made the trip home. My heart was giddy. I praised God for the breakthrough. Then my mind shifted to the three boys home alone for over two hours. Were they okay? What would the house look like? I wished I had time to call the other boy's mother before leaving. Driving slightly over the speed limit, I rolled into the drive. All the lights were on in the house, and I could hear laughter and yelling. Good. By the sound of things everyone was safe. They were enjoying the brief freedom from parental restrictions.

I called Andy to let him know I had arrived home safely. He would be home around 7:00 am. After corralling the boys and settling them into bed, I crawled into my own bed. Sighing with relief that Dad was in the hospital being cared for and the boys were safe, sleep arrived in short order.

The next morning I called the hospital. Dad had pneumonia. He would be getting IV antibiotics, then hopefully come home tomorrow. I then called Emma and gave her an update.

"I'll be there this week to help."

"Okay," I said, wondering how much help she would be. Although even a little help would be good, I always dreaded the possible confrontation or some untoward accusation. If a foul mood hit, she would lash out and pummel a cruel path of heartless words in my direction. I never quite knew how to defend myself. Avoiding her was my current feeble offense. Hopefully, all would be well with no contention.

The following day I drove to the hospital to pick up Dad. Thankfully he had escaped death and was breathing normally once again. He would be going home with oxygen. We stopped at the pharmacy and bought his antibiotics. Once home, we found Emma in Dad's apartment. She greeted Dad with a big bear hug, which he loved.

Emma did not have much to say to me. Her wild lifestyle left us with little in common. Tacit expectations for her favorite dinner of chicken and dumplings or meatloaf would be accommodated. Since she was looking after Dad, taking him out to lunch, and getting his groceries, I was more than happy to comply. Cooking was a creative outlet for me. I was able to hide in the kitchen and focus on the boys for a few days. I detached from Dad for a brief respite.

They made the way over to my house for dinners. Dad had weakened from the pneumonia and was using a walker. Emma brought beers for Andy, Dad and herself. She always brought me Diet Coke which I appreciated.

The dynamics changed when Emma visited. Her rebellious, yet entertaining personality demanded center stage. She was good-looking and quick witted with a joke that Dad could always hear. He was lighthearted and jovial in her company.

But I felt left out and somewhat rejected. I was amazed that she could show up for one week and get on the good side of Dad, which seemed to evaporate when she left.

As Dad declined, with the use of a walker and now oxygen, I thought the time was ripe to start Hospice. I was desperate for any help. The nurses would monitor his condition, and home health aides could help with showering.

Hospice also employed social workers who would come in and assess the needs of the caregiver and the patient. As individuals received the needed care, they often lived longer.

Since Dad was in good spirits, I decided to tell everyone before Emma left. I hoped to lessen tensions from the possibly unwelcome plan.

Mentally rehearsing my lines and all the possible outcomes, I took a deep breath, and determined to say what needed to be said, "I'm going to have Hospice come in."

BEFORE YOU DEPART

Emma quickly retorted, "You're just ready to bury him, aren't you? He told me he already made his funeral arrangements. Did you have anything to do with that? I don't see any benefit to Hospice or the death nurses coming. That's all they are. You must be in a real hurry to get all this over with."

Dad glared with his furrowed unibrow. "I don't think I'm ready for that."

The wall went up with thick tension. No discussion. Only negating a plausible suggestion. I opened my mouth to speak, but decided against contributing to further argument. I threw my hands up and left. Hot tears streamed down my face as I retreated to my house. I shook my head in disbelief at the bitter retort. I was angry and frustrated. My stomach roiled with nausea. I sank into our oversized couch.

Without saying goodbye, Emma left thirty minutes later. My idea had backfired. Her presence had made everything worse. Any peace between Dad and I was dashed in one brief conversation.

I felt heaviness and defeat combine with sudden exhaustion. Defying the weariness, I walked down the long drive-way and down the road. The fresh, cold air felt good.

I waited for Andy to wake up so I could vent about all the events of the day. In the meantime, I called Hospice.

BEFORE YOU DEPART

CHAPTER 5

My quiet time with the Lord continued to be the highlight of my days. God woke me up each morning. I felt an urging to meet with the God who knew all my desperate needs.

A friend had given me a 31-day devotional by Andrew Murray, *The Secret of Adoration.* As I read the daily devotion, God manifested His awe-inspiring presence.

His presence felt like a euphoric wave of peace, joy and love. The wave washed over me and lingered. I lost all connection with the world surrounding me. All tension left my body, and my whole being relaxed. I felt humbled as the worries fell away.

I fixated my thoughts on Almighty God, eager to know Him better. By the end of my devotion my heart was filled with worship. His desire was for me to come to Him, know Him and need Him. I could then face my day renewed, refreshed and hopeful.

This secret haven was a place reserved for only Him and me. I poured out my heart with seemingly impossible prayers. As the consuming wave washed over me I began to know what being one with the Lord Jesus meant. Nothing was more important than my time with Him. To search for Him and His enduring love and find it morning after morning.

BEFORE YOU DEPART

Prayers continued for reconciliation with Dad, salvation for Emma and the breaking of strongholds and family curses. After the confrontation of the previous day, I whispered more prayers for Emma.

The story of the biblical Joseph held special meaning. Joseph's life was full of tragedy and loss. Yet God used all the evil Satan intended for destruction, to eventually save the nation of Israel. If God could work in Joseph's life, He could certainly work in mine.

God demonstrated daily that the joy of the Lord was my strength. He was giving me deep understanding of scriptures that I had only read before. During my trials as caregiver, God was my constant companion and close friend.

While caring for Dad, I worried about homeschool. Yet God met our needs at every turn. I woke early and started school, this routine helped with productivity for myself and the boys. The goal was to finish school before anything happened or before the bull began to rage.

When he felt good, Dad was still able to venture out for lunch. Occasionally he brought home huge cinnamon rolls from Silver Dollar Café. The boys and I gathered for the treat. He also went to church which was something new. When we grew up he never went to church with my mother and me. I had always prayed for his salvation. Now I felt his church attendance was an answer to prayer.

On Saturdays we continued to take Dad out for lunch to one of his favorite eating spots. Andy was off work. Dad seemed to behave a little better when he was around. Dad always liked Andy's jokes, even if he had heard them before.

One day I asked, "Dad, are you mad at me?"

"No, Dolly, I just hurt all over."

We enjoyed going on field-trips. When he could, Dad went with us. One of Dad's favorite outings was an antique village reproduced. The antique exhibits included a church, homes, a doctor's office, dentist's office, livery stable and a gallows. Each establishment was filled with all the items of the time period. Stepping back in time was always one of my favorite things.

Since Dad was feeling good, he joined us on a trip to a turn-of-the-century working farm-turned museum. The farm held an annual spring festival with several craft booths including Dutch-oven cooking, soap-making, iron works aka the blacksmith, sorghum-rendering complete with the mule team and boiling vats used to refine the syrup.

The soap-making booth caught my eye. My grandmother had made soap out of necessity. I had inherited an old bar of soap she had decorated and a tin soap box for traveling. The items were treasures that helped me imagine Dad's world as a boy. They provided a feeling of connection to the past and a belonging to family. I barely knew my grandmother, but somehow these items provided an invisible link.

Dad enjoyed the sorghum-making. "I used to help the neighbor harvest and render sorghum. I think he gave me a gallon of sorghum for a day's work."

Andy said, "We have to buy some sorghum before we go."

Dad cheerfully said, "Today, the sorghums' on me."

Not willing to be left out, I replied, "I want some handmade soap." I rushed back to the booth to buy a handcrafted bar of soap and a book on soap-making.

We finished the day with lunch. The diversion was good for everyone.

Hospice came and admitted Dad, who offered no argument. The reality of death grew close once again, dampening Dad's good mood. He was quiet for a few days. I knew he was probably depressed.

Dad chose not to have the Hospice aide assist with showering. Instead she cleaned his small apartment. Dad's decline made washing his few dishes each day difficult.

The social worker must have been handpicked by God himself. I had an immediate connection with her. She listened, allowing me to pour out my frustrations, how I felt about Dad's anger and his rapid decline.

BEFORE YOU DEPART

When I finished, she gave me some suggestions. "Nanette, I want you to treat yourself to a haircut. Then do one other thing for yourself that might take your mind off things next door. Whatever you do, continue your daily walks."

"I didn't realize I looked so bad."

"You don't look bad. You just haven't been taking care of yourself. Most caregivers don't. Taking a little time for yourself would be good for you."

"I guess I have neglected myself. Other than grocery shopping, I hardly leave the house. I'm afraid Dad might fall or might need something or throw up and aspirate while I'm gone. I would hate to have the boys see that and me not be here."

"Yes, all that is a possibility, but everything you are worried about may not happen. You cannot control what happens if you leave. He still goes out for lunch if he feels good. So he'll probably be okay for two or three hours while you're gone."

My highlighted hair had long since grown out, showing gray roots. Six months had gone by and I had done nothing to my hair except pull it back into a ponytail.

"Okay, I'll do it." I was excited at the possibility of getting out by myself for a couple of hours. I felt relieved with the permission to get a haircut.

"I bought a book on soap-making. My grandmother used to make soap."

"Wonderful. That will give you a project to work on and the creative outlet would be great therapy. Make some soap soon."

I had to reassure myself that my small chaotic world would still be there when I came back. Certainly God was big enough to take care of everything without me. Dad would be okay for a short time, and I could ask a friend to take the boys for an afternoon.

The social worker validated my vulnerable emotions and shaky existence. Talking with someone about all I was going through had been a relief. I felt lighter, grateful to express the daily concerns and fears that fed into a subtle cloud of anxiety.

BEFORE YOU DEPART

As soon as the social worker left I set up the appointment for my haircut and made a list of supplies for my first batch of soap. I was grateful to be looking forward to something.

BEFORE YOU DEPART

CHAPTER 6

The outing for my haircut provided my desperate need for an emotional, energizing lift and brief respite. It rid me of the extra weight physically and emotionally. The short bob suited me.

My noon appointment coincided with Dad's daily outing time. I made quick stops for the soap-making supplies, then dashed home.

During the drive home, attempts to listen to Christian music and keep worries of Dad at bay failed. Mentally focusing on singing in my personal prayer language was more successful. The Holy Spirit provided a tune which continued all the way home. The melody was sweet and joyful, keeping thoughts of Dad's well-being to a minimum.

As I rolled in the drive with a pizza for dinner, all was well. Dad had a fine day, but was ready for a piece of deep dish supreme pizza. The boys chose the pepperoni.

Andy complimented my haircut, "Wow, I like that. You look better and look like you feel better." My reply was a brief carefree smile.

The short hiatus energized me. My mood was light and carefree. I chose not to focus on illness or school, but enjoyed the restful evening with Andy and the boys playing a game of Dominos.

BEFORE YOU DEPART

Mornings continued to be filled with the awe-inspiring presence of God. My devotional book focused on waiting for God and His glorious Holy Spirit. Each day led me in simple steps to humble myself, linger, and wait for the presence of God. He was always faithful to reward me with waves of grace, love, joy and that special peace that passed all understanding. My time with God increased my faith, ending in adoration for the God who was leading me through this blinding storm.

Pouring out my heart daily provided strength and grace for the day. Sometimes the song and tune the Holy Spirit gave repeated during my quiet time. Asking God for an interpretation ended in a beautiful song of praise. Adding guitar seemed to elevate the praise in my heart. The instrumentation followed more waves of loving embrace.

God was my sole source of refuge and solitude. A spiritual battle of unseen proportions raged. God alone knew the dire spiritual, physical and emotional needs of Dad, the family and myself. God alone could answer heartfelt, morning petitions.

The battle over the breaking of generational curses, reconciliations, fear, originally set up by Satan were not easily broken. Satan sent obstacles.

Ephesians 6:12 (NASB) reminded me the battle was against Satan:

"For our struggle is not against flesh and blood, but against the rulers, against the powers, against the world forces of this darkness, against the spiritual forces of wickedness in the heavenly places."

God provided His armor, protection and answer to prayer. But my participation was required through prayer, faith and obedience.

Friends could not relate with the caregiving situation and the sweeping range of emotions that flooded my bewildered heart. Most friends had grandparents younger than Dad. Nothing in their experience provided reference to the worries of caring for a loved one whose foot daily inched nearer to death's door. Andy helped all he could, but God alone knew my daily needs. He faithfully fulfilled them.

BEFORE YOU DEPART

The powerful morning quiet time was filled with hope that God would somehow answer the impossible pleas of reconciliation. The angry Ferdinand was ever ready to rage. Dad took all his anger out on me.

Hurting individuals hurt others. The social worker from Hospice said my dad probably felt safe venting anger toward me, because he knew I would still love him. That statement was true.

Still, his angry tone tore at my heart. Self-esteem suffered. *Was there anything that could please him? Did he still love me?* Subconsciously I knew Dad was miserable. But coping skills for the raging Ferdinand were limited.

One day Dad tried driving the tractor under some trees and almost fell off. He was angry, because the trees needed trimming.

Another day he asked me to buy gardening supplies so he could start his seeds indoors. I forgot, which caused another rage. "You never remember what I want. I'll get them myself." Guilt and confusion were constant companions as Dad pressed my emotional buttons.

At the same time, he was getting weaker and more forgetful. One day he came in and parked his car in the garage. But he left the motor running all night. Luckily there was enough oxygen to prevent carbon monoxide poisoning in his adjacent apartment.

The last time he drove his car was the day he approached his apartment too quickly and bumped the outside. Andy and I were tilling the garden. Dad did not back the car, but hurried into the apartment. We followed him to make sure he was okay. He was in the bathroom.

As he entered his small living room, Dad said, "I had to go the bathroom, Andy, and I couldn't wait."

Andy started laughing, "Are you okay?"

"Yes, much better now." We all laughed. No one was hurt. The dent in the shop was easily camouflaged by an antique metal swing.

The next morning over coffee Dad said, "I guess I'd better quit driving."

"Okay, if you think that's best." Thankfully I did not have to take the keys away. I can only imagine that fight.

All the small things in the daily routine added up. Waking up early, wondering how Dad was, making sure his light was on. Then coffee and the priceless quiet time, followed by school. Then the coffee break with Dad, keeping house, groceries for two households and preparing meals. Finding time for the boys in the middle of the rigid routine. Rolling into bed, checking to be sure Dad's lights were out.

Spring arrived and we planted the garden. We depended on the garden for most of our fresh vegetables which lowered our grocery bill. The garden was a family project. Andy plowed and tilled. Marty and Mitch helped. The squash seeds and tomato plants Dad started indoors were ready to be transplanted. We set up a chair for Dad so he could rest when needed. One of his frequent complaints was, "Dolly, I just can't do anything anymore."

Dad was a good gardener. Over the years he taught me how to build a compost pile and shared his techniques for success. We composted all our kitchen scraps, adding manure from the pasture. Dad insisted we gather all the grass cuttings and leaves possible, on the day he wanted it done. Nature did the rest.

The garden was looking good, including the asparagus sprouts planted earlier. They looked full and healthy. One day during the morning garden tour, the asparagus plants were all uprooted.

Disappointed and shocked, I shrieked, "What happened to the asparagus plants?"

Sheepishly Dad replied, "I thought they were weeds." He hung his head then chuckled apologetically.

Less than amused, I shook my head, but forced a fake smile. Discouraged at the waste of a good crop, my shoulders dropped. I diverted my attention to the tomatoes. Most of the time, negative emotions concerning Dad were buried. Any negative word was sure to end in an escalated rift. *He didn't mean to pull up something good. He was just trying to participate and be helpful.*

But the stuffed feelings of impatience, discouragement, and defeat were leading to a poisoned frame of mind. Powerless bitterness permeated the atmosphere. The steady, downward trajectory of disease, weakness and pending death surrounded Dad. The once gentle Ferdinand morphed more and more frequently into a raging bull.

My bitterness, fatigue and confusion simmered with a vengeful threat. Depression stifled the thunderous emotions in a volatile bottle of vulnerability.

Since Dad was no longer driving, he became dependent on me for his daily outing. One day he needed a haircut. As I dropped him off, I said, "The kids need to go to the library. We'll be back in just a little bit."

"Okay, Dolly."

In the library we hurried to pick out books, then rushed back to pick up Dad. He stood on the corner. Tension obvious in his shoulders, his stoic face and his stiff pace.

"Where have you been?" he bellowed.

"I told you we had to go to the library." Thankful for immediate heaven-sent response, we drove home in silence.

Piling out of the car, we headed into our separate domiciles. I grabbed the phone and called Dad's doctor. Sternly, I told the receptionist, "The doctor needs to give my dad something for his anger. I can't take this anymore. He takes all his frustrations out on me. I'm sick of it."

The receptionist quickly responded, "Have him make an appointment to see the doctor. We'll see what we can do."

Despite a growing headache, I made my way across the yard. The tension in my neck amplified. Neck pain and headaches seemed to happen more often. After relaying the message to Dad, he said, "Can you make the appointment for me? I can never hear the receptionist."

BEFORE YOU DEPART

The appointment made, I turned my attention to the soap supplies and my new project. I prayed for the relationship between Dad and me. Forgiveness and a clean heart free from the trappings of bitterness.

Intent intercession continued as I made the soap, a two-hour process. The warm soap mixture was poured into a cardboard box to finish the chemical reaction of saponification. Waiting for two weeks to cure before use seemed endless.

The wait on God to answer my prayer seemed even more remote. God held the keys to the miracle which seemed to drift farther away each day. The wall between Dad and me seemed to grow higher.

Time was running out. But giving up was not a choice.

BEFORE YOU DEPART

CHAPTER 7

Dad's new medicine was a wonder drug. An answer to prayer. The medication was Librium, a mood stabilizer used for anxiety. The gentle Ferdinand was back.

Something greater than the medication had taken place. *Did the doctor have a talk with him?* His attitude toward me changed. He was more grateful and patient. His tone held less sting. He was suddenly agreeable to afternoon appointments, so I could use mornings to finish home school.

My soap finished curing and I gave Dad a bar. He said, "Your soap sure is nice, Dolly. Your grandma used to make soap outside in a big black pot over the fire."

I smiled. My heart felt lighter as we enjoyed each other's company again. The invisible wall of defense built for pseudo protection began to crumble. My own bitterness melted away, and the feelings that I could do no right for him were edged out.

Joy came in other forms as well. In the evenings, the boys and I read aloud from *Rainbow Garden* by Patricia St John. The story was about a little girl who had to live with a family she did not know. The family introduced her to Christian values, scripture and prayer. The central theme of the story focused on the joy of the Lord. The scripture used was: *"You will show me the path of life; in Your presence is fullness of joy, at Your right hand are pleasures forevermore"* (Psalm 16:11 AMP).

One evening I shard the verse with Dad. He nodded in agreement that he liked it as well. I was grateful I could share my faith with him.

Dad continued to weaken. He spent more and more time in bed. If he ate, he threw up. For doctor appointments, he needed a wheelchair. One day we drove to one of our favorite restaurants. Andy had to carry him in.

Falls became frequent. I spent more time in Dad's apartment to ensure he had what he needed. Before going to bed, I laid my clothes out in case I needed to get up quickly. Some nights I slept in my clothes.

One day as Andy and I came home from a walk, we found Dad on the ground outside his apartment. He had taken a nitroglycerin tablet for chest pain and fell. I took his blood pressure and confirmed the nitroglycerin had made it drop too low.

Andy loaded Dad into the car and I drove him to the emergency room. By the time we arrived, his blood pressure had increased. They sent him home.

Dad's weakness and falls increased my obsessive worry. Headaches and neck pain amplified. Uncertainty and unease pervaded my mind. I was overprotective, not wanting to leave his apartment. Daily activities were performed in mindless, preoccupied anxiety. Buying groceries seemed a prolonged journey.

The social worker suggested, "Why don't you consider a respite for you and your Dad. Put him in the nursing home for a few days. Hospice will pay."

My immediate reply was, "How can I do that to him?"

"How long can you keep doing this caregiving? You aren't sleeping well. The next step is sleeping at your Dad's apartment. Since he doesn't hear, he's probably pretty noisy."

Laughing in agreement, I said, "Yes, he's pretty noisy alright."

BEFORE YOU DEPART

Emma came for a visit. The break she provided was nice. I slept better knowing someone was with Dad. I kept to myself, baked some cookies and made a batch of soap.

Dad was having difficulty walking ten feet into the bathroom. One day Emma said, "Do you think he's really having that much difficulty? Is your Dad faking or falling for attention?"

In disbelief, I said, "No, I don't think so." I walked out and hoped Dad would be okay in my absence.

One morning the boys and I joined Dad and Emma for a coffee break. Dad lay on the floor while Emma watched him try to get up.

The boys and I picked his thin, weak frame from the floor. "Are you hurt?"

"No, Dolly, but I've fallen and can't get up." We laughed, because he sounded like the Life Alert commercial.

Turning to Emma with a flash of anger, I said, "He is not faking it. Falls can be serious for older people. What if he breaks something? I thought you were here to help him."

My tendency to control everything, including falls, contradicted Emma's cavalier approach to Dad's care. The control led to frustration and anger with present and past situations. My fierce need to cling to an illusion of perfection led to increased fatigue and depression. Being a nurse didn't help. The textbook fantasy conjured in my imagination would never exist in the present nightmare. Helplessness was the pervading miasma as I watched Dad's spiraling trajectory of health decline a little at a time.

Occasionally there was a conflicting, haunting thought. *How long can I do this? How long can Dad do this? How much weaker can he get? He's like the Energizer Bunny that keeps on going and going.* Giving up had never been an option for Ferdinand the Bull and Dad's present condition was no different. Cancer of the esophagus was just another obstacle to overcome. Dad would defy the odds as long as he could.

BEFORE YOU DEPART

Emma seemed extra reclusive during this visit. Attempting to be amiable, I made her favorite dinner of chicken and dumplings.

The nursing home was making more and more sense. Tonight might be a good time to mention a short respite.

Dad and Emma came over for dinner. When Dad left, I motioned for Emma to stay. Prayed for sustained peace.

"I've been thinking of putting Dad in a nursing home for a short stay. Hospice will pay for it."

Emma retorted, "You just can't wait for this to be over. Are you trying to rush things by putting him in a nursing home that won't take care of him?"

With a God-given calm, I replied, "You're not here all the time, Emma. He's getting weaker by the day and falling more. I can't even leave to get groceries. I'm afraid to go over to my house and check on the boys for fear something might happen."

Emma left in a bitter rush. Her usual heated reaction, poor listening skills and inability to discuss anything in a rational manner had not changed. She did not want Dad in the nursing home any more than I did.

The decision made, I notified the nursing home. They had a private room available. The doctor was nearby. Two of Dad's friends lived nearby and could visit. A thirty-minute drive wasn't too far for me.

The social worker from Hospice agreed to provide moral support as I delivered the news to Dad and Emma. We walked to Dad's apartment, not knowing what to expect.

Anger flashed in Dad's eyes as he yelled, "I took care of you when you weighed three pounds and three ounces."

He said more, but I couldn't comprehend the words. Hot tears of guilt welled up. The nursing home was a bad idea. Familiar rejection and defeat crowded my thoughts.

Unwilling to hear anymore, I couldn't leave fast enough, but was unable to escape the anger and despair. The social worker stayed behind. She came

BEFORE YOU DEPART

to the house later and said, "I told him to be ready by nine tomorrow morning." She stayed until everyone calmed down.

My birth had come two months premature, and my weight had been a mere three pounds and three ounces. Obviously, I had been a burden and worried Dad, but I never knew. Now I was abandoning him to the dreaded nursing home. Anger rose in my chest, resentful of the difficult decision that had to be made.

Everyone would blame me.

Would Dad forgive me for this unspeakable act of abandonment? This would probably be the final wedge between Emma and me. Any ground I had gained with Dad would certainly be lost. Things had been good for the last few weeks. How could God provide what I so desperately needed from Dad?

Thankfully Andy supported my decision. He knew how helpless I felt.

The next morning, I trudged over to Dad's place. He was busy packing his few belongings.

With sad Ferdinand eyes he looked at me. "I don't want to go." He started crying. No anger in his eyes, only a fear I had never witnessed in my forty years. My heart tore. For a brief moment I thought, *maybe we could make this work. Somehow.*

Godly strength rose up to help me do what had to be done. Never before able to stand up to Dad, my back became erect. I stated the ultimate boundary. With a stern voice, I said, "I don't see any way around this decision." All the while my heart wrenched at the awful deed about to be done.

Emma came to the house shortly after to tell me Dad was ready. She too had conceded with my stern command.

Together we loaded Dad. The kids also rode along. We traveled in silence, each searching for a different scenario to the dreaded destination that lay ahead.

BEFORE YOU DEPART

We were met by the matronly administrator who showed us the way to Dad's room. The repugnant hallways were exactly as I remembered. The repulsive nursing home smell accosted my senses. Subconsciously scanning the environment, I noted the floor was spotless. All seemed clean, yet a horrendous smell of urine filled the atmosphere. *How could two opposites exist in the same building?* I didn't want to know.

The tears we had all been holding back roiled to the surface. Emma walked to the car with the kids. Her frame bent in sorrow and defeat, sobbing with uncontrollable heaves.

I turned to the kind administrator who was close to tears. Her attempts to calm me failed. "I can't leave him here."

The small, feisty matron replied with understanding brown eyes, "We'll take good care of your father. Just try it for one night."

I nodded in obedience as tears and snot rolled down my face.

We rode home in a trance of grieved shock. Sobs filled the car. Tissues passed around. We wept like small abandoned children suffering from separation anxiety.

Why did it have to be this way? Why did all of this have to happen? Was it right to put him where his parents had been? What would I do with all my idle time now that Dad had been put away?

The harsh reality of pending death permeated the atmosphere. The spectral reality pressed in from all sides. I felt as if I might suffocate.

That evening I sat in the dark, immobilized by guilt and grief. No tears left. Dad had been abandoned to his worst nightmare. All my fault. Now I would have to witness the horrendous consequences.

Would he still love me? Would he be mad? Would he ever forgive me? Would God be able to deliver my heart's cry for a daughter-father reconciliation? Was all lost?

I woke up on the couch, my clothes rumpled from sleep. The anguish and guilt returned like a harassing demon as I remembered the previous day. The worst day of my life.

BEFORE YOU DEPART

CHAPTER 8

My clothes were rumpled from falling asleep on the couch. Disoriented from waking in a foreign spot, I quickly remembered last night.

The feat had been accomplished. Dad was now in a nursing home. This was where independence whittled away. With no control over what I had done, how did Dad feel? He could no longer ask for a simple egg-over-easy like he did at home.

Dad no longer slept in his own bed. This bed was assigned, and he had few belongings of his own. He now depended on strangers to provide his care instead of Emma or me.

The guilt resumed. *Was this best for me or for Dad?*

He begged to stay home, but Dad was now in a holding cell for the elderly. His clothes monogramed with a Sharpie. In congregate care, he would eat what was served, rise and retire at the institution's designated time.

Recently Dad told me, "I look in the mirror and I don't even recognize myself."

My forty-year-old self could not relate. *Maybe you should just be grateful to be alive.* But yes, he had aged.

Emma left without saying goodbye. Another grief out of my control. Following all the disagreements over Dad, would our relationship ever mend?

BEFORE YOU DEPART

My heart felt like lead and my shoulders slumped. My body was heavy as I dragged myself off the couch. I needed to go see how Dad was tolerating his new home.

When the boys and I arrived, Dad was quiet and withdrawn. He took his meals in his room, refusing to eat in the dining room. His decision did not surprise me. One time I asked Dad why he never went to the Senior Citizen's meal in town. He said, "I don't like being around all those old people."

The matronly administrator came in and assured me all was fine. Dad would adjust. She took me to the nursing station and introduced me to the staff. They all seemed pleasant and genuinely interested in Dad's care.

The nurse for the day shift was a portly, gray-haired woman with a warm smile. She reported that Dad slept well. Yesterday was a good day. . The energetic activities director wore an infectious smile, pausing briefly to introduce herself. She was young and obviously loved her job.

"Dad likes his morning paper," I said.

Her enthusiastic reply, "I'll make sure he gets one every day."

During the summer months, we ventured daily to the nursing home. The boys and I maintained the garden. Dad's squash produced a bumper crop. One day we stopped by a produce stand, and I sold all the squash. The vendor bought it by the pound, twenty dollars' worth.

When I told Dad the news, he chuckled. "That reminds me of the fruit stand when we sold peaches and pears. I'm glad you were able to sell the produce instead of throwing it away."

"Me, too. The lady pays me by the pound, and squash weighs a lot. She even buys the really big ones."

One day, Dad was agitated. He didn't have any clothes on and was tangled up in his covers. He bellowed, "Come in here!"

Calling for the nurse, I cautiously walked in. Thankfully the nurse came quickly and helped him. I uttered a prayer to God that he would be okay, glad the responsibility of calming him down was not mine.

BEFORE YOU DEPART

My muscles tensed in retreat to the common room. My desire was to be his daughter, not his nurse.

Being his nurse would take the daughter role to a level I did not want. The nursing role involved cleaning up vomit or diarrhea when he couldn't make it to the bathroom. Bathing him when he became too weak to bathe himself. Seeing his naked, weakened frame would shatter my fantasy of faux vitality and uncover this vulnerable, feeble man.

Perhaps the child residing within could not come to terms with the stark reality. Was it my way of keeping him as my father while holding on to some feeble denial that he would remain continent and healthy? My piece of reality needed the dignity of my not caring for him.

Caring for the elderly is a noble calling. Caring for others as they approach death is a privilege. Nursing others to whom one is not related provides an imaginary buffer, a boundary to the finality of the death experience. Watching the pain of those nearing death generates a compassion to help and assist, devoid of complete immersion into the experience.

But caring for my father would only add to my already overwhelming pain. Allowing others to care for him allowed me to deny his next decline toward helplessness. My need was to hold Dad in the ever capable role of a father who would do anything in his power for me—for all time.

To nurse him would negate the fragile denial of mortality. Intimate care would also add to my resentment. The elderly state of weakness would eventually consume the Dad I adored and nullify the deity I afforded him as a small child.

When they settled Dad, the nurse came for me. He was quieter than usual. His television volume was loud, which the nurse said bothered the other residents. His hearing aids did little to amplify sound. For a short time, we watched TV together.

BEFORE YOU DEPART

Dad had given up playing Solitaire. The television was one of his few enjoyments along with the newspaper. Perhaps we could find some ear phones.

Dad spoke up, "I want to go for a ride. Let's go get some ice cream. I want a vanilla shake."

"Okay, let's go."

We wheeled him out and into the car. The errand was short. He seemed satisfied with a drive around town to the local Braums. He ordered his vanilla shake, while I ate my usual twist cone.

Later, as I was about to leave the nursing home, Dad said, "Dolly, call the nurse. I don't feel very good."

His feet were turning purple, and the maleficent color seemed to be traveling up his body.

Running to the nurse's station, I said, "Come quick. Dad is turning blue."

The nurse hurried in. "I'll call the doctor and see if we can get him some morphine. That may help." Morphine would dilate the blood vessels and hopefully restore any impaired circulation.

Relinquishing any nursing decision or judgment, I nodded in anxious agreement. I had never seen such symptoms before, and Dad's breathing looked okay. I gave him a kiss so they could work on him. Then I left.

Praying all the way home, I wondered, *would he be okay? He was so blue. God please take special care of my dad. I'm not ready for him to go.*

Pulling into the drive, I raced into the house and called the nursing home. "Is Dad okay?"

"Yes, his color returned to normal after we gave him the morphine. He's sleeping now."

Relieved, my prayers continued for all my impossible requests. *Time is running out. What if he dies before my prayer is answered? The reconciliation hasn't happened yet. How could it when he's deaf and doesn't know my desperate need. God has to intervene. The hope for my necessary*

BEFORE YOU DEPART

miracle seems transient and unattainable. Is God listening? He promised to hear my prayer.

Persistent prayer brought back the glimmer of hope that God would deliver my nameless miracle before Dad died.

BEFORE YOU DEPART

BEFORE YOU DEPART

CHAPTER 9

At times the emotional tug of war toggled toward bitterness. The losing battle ended in a mire of self-pity fueled by thoughts of what might have been. If only Dad was younger. If only he hadn't gotten sick.

My boys were forever cheated from knowing the younger version of Dad. The grandfather who loved to play catch. Their doting grandfather absent from sports events, home runs and touchdowns of future games. Dad would miss their weddings and the birth of their children.

I fought the bitterness with prayer and forgiveness. My thoughts teetered toward gratitude. God answered my prayer as a little girl by not letting him die. My child-mind knew he was older. I feared losing him at a tender age.

Gratitude settled in. My boys did *know* their grandfather and had a relationship with him.

Summer passed. Home school needed to resume. We belonged to a home school co-op that offered a science class in Owasso, Oklahoma. Just enough time to make the forty-five minute drive to the nursing home, visit Dad, and then travel back.

The drive provided time to pray. Desperate prayer for Dad and the inconsolable, intangible request that nagged deep in my soul. Emma's salvation topped the list. My personal prayer language took over with fervency as English words seemed empty and powerless.

Spiritual warfare was on the forefront. Satan devised principalities and powers concerning my family, Dad and me. Family curses operated in the form of depression and victimization. All these invisible entities must be dealt with before Dad departed. My prayers were urgent and insistent, often bringing me to tears. Loud cries filled my car as I screamed at Satan who had come to cheat, lie, steal and destroy. Only Christ could overcome his power.

Singing in the spirit was part of my routine. Recurrent tunes filled the drive. Bitterness was held at bay for another day. Hope returned that God might possibly answer my prayers.

Dad's birthday was approaching. Maybe a letter in his birthday card would bridge the divide in our relationship.

Dear Dad,

I sure do love you the mostest. I want you to know how much I loved growing up in Littlerock, California, helping in the peach and pear harvest. I also enjoyed how you moved with me to Oklahoma my first year of college and stayed with me. We had fun. It was great being able to walk to Braums for an ice cream after dinner. I remember you always got buttered pecan, and I got a pistachio sundae. Yum. Thank you for teaching me to prune the peach trees. I know you didn't feel good.

Let's go get some ice cream today for your birthday.

Love you the mostest,

Nanette

When I gave him his card, he said, "I love you too, Dolly. Let's go get an ice cream."

He could no longer walk to the car. I helped him into a wheelchair and wheeled him out. He could still stand and get in the car. He ordered the usual vanilla shake, while I ate my usual vanilla-chocolate twist yogurt cone.

BEFORE YOU DEPART

On the way home tears flowed. Dad's reaction to my letter was nice, but not what I expected or needed. Maybe my expectations were too high. The disappointment of an unfulfilled need took over and left me despondent.

How could he be reached other than a letter? He couldn't hear well enough to carry on a conversation. Was Dad punishing me?

Maybe what I needed didn't even exist. The response required something deeper. But what was the response my soul craved?

What if he never responded and just slipped away. What if all of my attempts to reach him failed? What if God never answered my desperate pleas?

The only good thing about a terminal diagnosis is the blessing of a goodbye and the chance to mend fences. That blessing happened with Mom.

Before she died I wrote a thank you letter. She really liked it.

My letter was full of gratitude for all the things she taught me: making peach cobbler, the best cookies ever, and nurturing my faith after accepting Jesus into my heart. Her influence touched my life in many ways.

But Dad was different. The gentle Ferdinand still had a bullish exterior. Hopefulness dwindled once again. Dad's time grew shorter. He was getting weaker. His emaciated frame bore eighty pounds.

My trips to the nursing home dwindled to two or three times a week. Going more frequently stressed our home school routine. The boys visited Dad with me. Sometimes Andy went and afterward we went out for dinner. Dad usually did not want to go. When asked, he said, "No. I'll just throw up the food anyway."

One of my worries centered on how the boys were handling everything. Laurie, a friend who also home schooled her children, reassured me that life was school, and school was life. As we took care of Dad, the boys learned valuable life lessons.

One Saturday, Laurie called, "How's your Dad?"

"He's not doing very well. He throws up most of his food and is losing more weight." Crying, I continued. "He seems so distant. He can't hear anything I say. I keep praying for a break-through in our relationship, but I don't know what to do."

"Write your dad a letter. You like to write."

"I just wrote him a letter and nothing happened."

"Write him again."

Laurie was like Jesus with skin on. Her call was an answer to prayer.

I started another letter. *What could I say?* I prayed for help.

Dear Dad,

I sure do love you. I tried to pick pears as fast as you did, but I never could. I liked the year you and I did the U-Pick Pear Operation together, and you gave me half of everything we earned. That made me feel grown up. Growing up in Littlerock, California was great. I can't imagine growing up any other way.

When I was little you sometimes seemed sad. I always wanted to fix it and make you happy. But it's not possible for me to fix anything. Not when I was little and not now. Only Jesus Christ of Nazareth can do that. He knows what you need, and He is able to do it. He loves you and God is your Heavenly Father. I love you, too.

Love you the mostest,

Nanette

As Dad finished the letter, he said "Come here, Dolly." He was in bed, but he pulled me close and gave me a hug. A hug like he used to give me. Tears of gratitude rolled down my cheeks. The hug seemed to melt any malice between us. We hugged for what must have been two hours. Tears of relief poured out. The hug was like a token love. My prayer was answered better than I could think or ask.

Dad patted my shoulders, "What's wrong, Dolly?"

"I'm going to miss you. I wish you didn't have to go."

"I'm going to miss you, too."

Several minutes passed, then I said, "I love you."

"I love you, too, Dolly."

BEFORE YOU DEPART

The drive home was filled with relief, praise, and gratitude that Dad had responded in such a wonderful way. My attention was diverted to the beautiful trees which were just beginning to show the change of season as they gave way to fall colors.

The hugs continued. The nurses would come and go, smiling warmly. They liked Dad and were always willing to give me an update on his condition.

Thanksgiving and Christmas approached. Prayers continued with the added plea, "Don't let him die during the holidays."

BEFORE YOU DEPART

BEFORE YOU DEPART

CHAPTER 10

Dad kept giving his everlasting hugs. My prayers continued with vigilance. I longed to grasp all God might give in this chaotic storm of illness. New songs permeated my spirit to and from the nursing home.

Fall arrived with cooler temperatures, changing leaves and an opportunity to attend a ladies' retreat in Hot Springs, Arkansas. Several friends and I had attended faithfully the last fifteen years.

A three-day weekend away with friends on a spiritual retreat sounded great. *Dare I leave Dad? What if he died while I was gone? Would worry and obsession over Dad ruin my trip?*

Wondering if I should chance leaving, I called Laurie. "Do you think I should leave my dad for three days?"

Laurie said, "I'll be praying for your decision. If you go, I'll pray that you get exactly what you need."

I made the decision to attend the retreat. I would leave the number of retreat center with my husband and the nursing home. They could call me if Dad's condition declined. Worst case scenario, I would have to turn around and head home.

BEFORE YOU DEPART

The retreat was held at a rustic children's church camp. We slept in the children's cabins on bunk beds. With the focus on Jesus, none of us minded the rustic amenities. They fed us great hearty meals. I felt nurtured in body, rested in mind and revitalized spiritually.

The subject to be studied was always a surprise. This year's theme turned out to be putting Christ back in Christmas and the spiritual reason we celebrate Thanksgiving.

The minister made the story come to life. She relied heavily on visual stimulation, drawing us into the teaching as if we were witnesses. Mary rode on a donkey. She and Joseph made their journey down the hill. At their journey's end was a living nativity in the town of Bethlehem. The story of the first Christmas unfolded before us. The night was cold, adding to the aesthetics. The angst Mary must have felt as she brought Jesus our Savior into the world in the humble stable surroundings.

At the conclusion of the weekend, we were given the challenge to make Jesus' birth real and fresh in our families. And the minister charged us with keeping the story alive for the next generation.

We received several ideas and references on how to make the holidays come to life. Peter Marshall's account of the Pilgrims in *The Light and the Glory* was the recommendation for a historical reference. Perfect for homeschool in the coming weeks.

On my return home, my fears were allayed once again. God graciously took care of Dad during my absence.

Delving into the quest to make the holidays special was fueled by renewed faith and purpose. Worries over Dad's condition were overshadowed by something greater. My spirit was energized by joy and refreshed with reminders of the love of God who took on flesh to be Emanuel, God with us. The baby Jesus who would take away the sins of the world.

Fueling my excitement for the mission ahead, I already owned *The Light and the Glory*. We had never read it. All I needed was one more book. Emily

BEFORE YOU DEPART

Barnes had written a book about Christmas memories, but it was nowhere to be found in the library system. Our current finances prohibited the purchase of the book.

One day at a homeschool ice skating outing in Tulsa, I happened to sit by Jessica. We were acquainted but had never talked. Conversing about the seminar and the book, I said, "I've looked all over for an Emily Barnes book. I can't find it anywhere."

Jessica said, "I have that book in my car. You can have it. I'll run out and get it."

In awe, I thanked her. Amazed by God's touch in my circumstances increased my faith. He provided once again, attending to each detail. God's providential hand filled my needs as the holidays approached.

Projects for Thanksgiving and reading *The Light and the Glory* filled our homeschool day. The boys decorated napkin rings made out of paper towel rolls. My creative outlet satiated through making place settings for each of us with a scripture to be read for the meal blessing.

Andy didn't have to work on Thanksgiving that year, which was unusual. That morning he and the boys headed outside for a deer hunt. During their absence I quickly set the table and finished preparing the meal.

For the first time in eighteen years, I used my wedding dishes. They had been tucked away after our first Thanksgiving meal attempt as a married couple. That day was dashed by an aunt who refused my invitation because my house was too small to accommodate her personal liking. I allowed the rejection to wound me for future celebrations. Not this year. Forgiveness was on the menu for her and anyone else making an attempt to condemn or judge.

Andy and the boys returned from their hunt. No deer, but the table was set to perfection. Candles included. Each plate held five kernels of corn to remember the Pilgrims' first harsh winter of rationing and near starvation. The meal ended in a Thanksgiving communion with sparkling grape juice. The best Thanksgiving ever.

BEFORE YOU DEPART

We took leftovers to Dad and spoke a prayer over him. He liked the sweets best. I included slices of mincemeat and pumpkin pie.

Next came Christmas.

My goal was to keep the focus on Jesus' birth, not the overshadowing of Dad's illness. Homemade decorations topped the agenda. Name settings created, complete with Christmas scriptures.

Emma came for a visit. My anxiety increased. *What would happen this time? She always created strife of some kind.*

She kept to herself and visited Dad every day. My hugs ceased when she came, changing the dynamics between Dad and me. The message came through loud and clear that she was here to visit Dad, not me. I had to remember my stance to forgive and allow the grace of God to work, should He choose to do that.

Christmas morning arrived. Emma declined my invitation to Christmas dinner, saying she would eat with Dad.

Snow started to fall, but Emma insisted on seeing Dad. The wintery precipitation covered the ground in white flurries. Accumulations greater than predicted on weather reports.

Emma called near noon, "Can I still come to your dinner?"

"Sure." I hurriedly made a place setting for Emma, complete with her part of the Christmas story prayer.

She arrived an hour later. Snow slowed the thirty-minute drive. Unable to traverse the hill on the driveway, she got stuck and walked up the hill.

We gathered for dinner. Everyone including Emma read their prayer. She smiled as she read. Something had changed. She wasn't her normal cynical self in regard to the prayer or participation. No sarcasm or derogatory remarks.

My heart thrilled at the touch of God once again. He had answered another impossible prayer, touching Emma's heart. Worship flowed in silent prayer. Our Christmas celebration turned out to be a perfect day. God's presence filled the room with peace and joy. Retreating to the bathroom, tears of gratitude and joy flowed.

My imagination stretched for answers. *Did Dad's minister talk to Emma?*

He was a precious man of God. When Dad was diagnosed, he came for a visit. I asked him, "Do you think Dad has asked Jesus into his heart and received Him as his Savior?'

He answered, "God knows His sheep, and your Dad is certainly one of them."

Emma surprised me again that evening. Coming back for seconds on pie, she isolated me. She said, "I sure am thankful for all you've done for Dad."

"I wish I could have kept him home longer. But I think the nursing home is keeping a close eye on him."

"He can be difficult sometimes. I know it's been hard."

"Sometimes, but we're making it."

Lying down for bed that night, sleep evaded me. Energized by the amazing events of the day left me with feelings of euphoria. Joy-filled tears rolled down my cheeks.

God had answered all my prayers. I had my reconciliation from Dad. He had not passed during the holidays. Emma's heart had softened. Emma had even thanked me for all my efforts.

God was answering all my prayers out of the richness of His grace and glory. He was taking care of every detail, doting each "i," and crossing every "t."

BEFORE YOU DEPART

CHAPTER 11

The spirit of Christmas extended beyond December 25th. Christmas leftovers filled our stomachs and Emmanuel, God with us, filled my heart. God answered my prayers throughout the holiday season. My efforts to emphasize Christ during Thanksgiving and Christmas were successful beyond expectation. God's hand evident through inexplicable touches.

The heavy snow made travel difficult for two days. Despite travel advisories, Emma left the day after Christmas.

The roads were too hazardous for Andy to deliver gas in the eighteen-wheeler. We still needed to deliver Dad's Christmas present. I was anxious to see how he liked his gift. Cabin fever and restlessness overcame caution as Andy drove us to the nursing home.

Dad always told a story of how he lost his ice skates. In the early 1900's, the winters were cold and harsh, making the ponds safe for skating. Dad and his two older brothers ventured out to skate on the frozen pond. Somehow he came home without his skates. His ice skating adventures ceased for that winter.

BEFORE YOU DEPART

A search in the local antique shops for a pair of ice skates made my shopping complete. We gave Dad his present, tied together with red ribbon. He chuckled, "You found my skates." We also took him a piece of pumpkin bread.

Stopping by the nurses' station, I asked, "How is he doing?" Always cheerful and glad to see me, Janie, the day nurse said, "He's not eating much and what he does eat he throws up."

His appearance was frail and emaciated. His strength diminished, he now used a bed side commode so he wouldn't have to walk to the bathroom.

One week after Christmas he got the flu and was admitted to the hospital. The doctor warned us, "He may not pull through."

Once again I braced myself for the worst. The emotional roller coaster included dread of his final demise. I called Emma, but she couldn't come.

Dad's Energizer Bunny kicked in again. The determined Ferdinand rallied. He left the hospital feeling better than prior to his illness. For two weeks he was able to get up and use his walker to make it to the bathroom. Thankful, I increased my visits.

Since Dad was holding his own, I enrolled in a Master Gardener Class at the local, Oklahoma Extension Office. I had always wanted to take that class. It was once a week for four hours which wouldn't take much time. I took the chance, hoping Dad would continue in his current energized state.

Dad's health concerns and ever-pending death resulted in my caution to add anything extra to my plate. The class would give me something to look forward to and distract me from Dad's decline.

But the following week Dad stopped eating. He was still able to drink. He had to use the bed side commode. When I went to see him, we held hands. The hugs had stopped, but the gentle Ferdinand remained alert, making eye contact.

Janie, the nurse said, "He's drinking sips, but soon that will stop. When a person is nearing death, the body gradually shuts down. He's too weak to digest food. All his energy is going to his heart and lungs to keep him alive."

BEFORE YOU DEPART

"How long do you think it will be?"

"It's different with everyone. Dying individuals usually last about one or two weeks after they stop eating and drinking. But only God knows for sure."

Turning my attention back to Dad, he kept saying, "I love you the mostest, Dolly."

Through my tears, I replied loudly, "No you don't. I love *you* the mostest."

Our simple conversation never grew old. The entire hall could hear, despite the door being closed. I wanted to say it one more time, not knowing when the last time would be.

One night the nursing home called. Judy, the night nurse said, "He's getting close to dying. You'd better come in. He has Cheyne-Stokes breathing."

"Okay, I'm on my way."

Often seen before death, Cheyne Stokes breathing is irregular and agonizing to witness. Breathing is progressively deep, followed by short shallow breaths then a pause in breathing called apnea. The breathing pattern cycles approximately every thirty seconds to two minutes. Apneic episodes become longer and longer until the last breath is drawn.

On my way to the nursing home I notified Emma. Upon arrival, Dad whispered, "Hi Dolly, I love you the mostest." He was quiet, motionless. The only movement was a mysterious reaching to some invisible something.

What was he seeing? Loved ones who had already passed? Jesus, waiting to take him home?

Through my tears, I replied, "I love you the mostest." We held hands, his grasp weak.

Emma arrived later. The nurse brought us some chairs and said, "You can spend the night if you want. I also brought you some blankets."

We sat beside Dad. Thick tension still continued between Emma and me. Enduring an uncomfortable silence as long as possible concluded in my decision to leave. I wanted Dad to myself. This could be my last chance to be with him. Holding back tears in Emma's presence, my lips touched his forehead. "I'll see you in the morning, Dad." No reply.

Disappointed and resentful about the heavy atmosphere, I walked toward the door. Emma left when I did.

Certainly Dad's Energizer Bunny would kick in one last time. Surely my thoughts and prayers would will him to make it until I returned. Tired and weary over undulating emotions of grief and resentment, I drove home and fell into fitful sleep.

Waking with a flinch, the memory of the previous night careened into consciousness. The nursing home had not called. He was still alive. I could see him one more time.

Determination to make it to the nursing home hastened my sluggish pace. Dressed in last night's clothes and with uncombed hair, my drive was halted halfway by Janie's call, "Your dad just died."

Crying, I stopped the car along the side of the road and called Andy, then Emma.

Imploding disappointment, failure and guilt flooded my already weary mind, haunting me. He died alone. *I wanted to be there when he died. I should have stayed at the nursing home all night. I abandoned him on his last night of life. The nursing home even called because they didn't want him to die alone. Certainly I could have tolerated an uncomfortable chair and Emma's tension. Why didn't I get out of bed earlier?*

Rueful tears fell accompanied by gut-wrenching sobs. My deepest regret met me with the sight of Dad's lifeless body.

Janie said, "I had the nurse call you last evening so you could be with him. I thought you would stay last night."

My guilty reply. "Yes, I know. I wish I had stayed." I had no excuse.

This visit was short. The shell of his body devoid of spirit could no longer interact or tell me he loved me. The long awaited harsh reality of death had arrived.

BEFORE YOU DEPART

Gathering a few belongings Dad no longer needed, I left. Janie gave me a warm hug. The nurses had witnessed our journey. They grieved Dad's final day and my loss.

As I backed my car out of the lot, Emma pulled up. I waved, but pulled away. My car's slow motion matched my emotions. My goodbye complete, Emma could have her time with Dad.

Although I relished the seclusion on my drive home, the reality of Dad's death hit me. Emotions oscillated from sadness, sorrow, disbelief, and devastation to a deep chasm of grief.

One emotion included relief that his suffering had ended. Relief that nursing home visits were no longer necessary. Those feelings of relief melted into guilt.

At home, I looked at the funeral home folder of prearranged instructions. Called the minister. He came to the house that afternoon and we discussed Dad's wishes.

He was kind and loving with a welcoming demeanor. Talking about Dad, he said, "I visited your Dad about once every week or two while he was in the nursing home."

"That's great. He always told me he never had any visitors."

Smiling he said, "Sometimes I took Ruby with me." Ruby was one of Dad's childhood friends.

"I shared one of my favorite verses with Dad. He seemed to like it. Psalm 16:11."

"Okay, I'll use that whole chapter for the message."

Next on the list of dreaded duties was calling the funeral home. The attendant gently guided me through the proceedings, and we set the date for Dad's burial. Dad had prearranged everything, including the hymns he wanted to be sung.

Grateful he had asserted his wishes, I now knew more about him.

Next on the agenda was notifying all his friends. Few were living. In his address book, Dad had marked through the ones who were deceased. Many were lifelong friends, my friends included. They all loved him. He called them all Dolly and made them feel special.

The day of the funeral arrived. Dad had arranged for a graveside service. Fitting for a funeral, the day was cold, dreary, and rainy. Three of my friends attended while others sent flowers. Emma chose not to attend the sparse gathering.

Dad was the last of five brothers to be laid to rest in the Welch cemetery. All lay in a row. His mother, father, grandfather and grandmother already buried.

Were they all together in heaven?

As we journeyed through the cemetery to the burial site, I said, "Dad was the last of the Martin boys. Now he's gone, too."

Ruby let out a gasp of grief.

Afterward everyone came to our house for lunch. We talked about Dad. Cindy, my friend from college said, "Your dad was so sweet. Even though he wasn't a big man, he seemed like a gentle giant. He always had a twinkle in his eye. He was kind of mysterious though, because he was so quiet. He had such a love and concern for you that was so evident. You had a good Dad."

Laurie said, "I loved the faithful loyalty and friendship that your dad had with me and my parents."

Andy said, "He was like the dad I never had. We may have butted heads a few times but we were always able to resolve it. That strengthened the relationship. I appreciated that. I liked making him laugh."

Soon everyone left. Except for Andy and the boys, an emptiness permeated the room. The tacit shadow of grief fell like fog.

My grief remained, leaving me to search for the missing piece no longer to be found.

CHAPTER 12

A short hiatus of joy quelled the approaching wall cloud of grief. God's answers to all my wistful prayers carried me on a carefree spiritual cloud. The retelling of the events of the stormy year and God's orchestration of each detail of Dad's death galvanized my faith.

The Master Gardener Course continued. Wanting to share my skills, I taught a botany class for the homeschool co-op.

Then the reality of Dad's death hit.

Everyone had heard the story of God's touch the final year before Dad died. Conversations did not and could not include grief. The tacit rule to just "Get over my grief" came into play.

Isolation crept in, accompanied by anger and resentment. Grief seemed to be an intolerable emotional state. Well-meaning friends told me to pray through the feelings of loss. "Time will heal the hurt."

But how much time?

God was silent. The waves of His loving kindness and presence ceased.

Extreme exhaustion debilitated me. Sleepless, endless nights dragged out.

BEFORE YOU DEPART

The reality of Dad's death surrounded me. The endless evasion of pending death was over. The continual trajectory of declining health ended. Dad was gone. He would not return.

My grief encompassed all previous losses. Extended family were all dead. My mother's side of the family had one living sibling out of thirteen. All uncles deceased from Dad's side of the family.

At forty, I was an orphan.

Dad was the last of a dying generation. The last of those shaped by the Great Depression. A generation known for concrete values who knew right and wrong. No need to lock doors in his time. His family was well-known and respected in the small community of Welch.

He witnessed the horse and buggy give way to the automobile. Then air travel and space travel. Dad was a fine representative of a hardworking lost generation.

The gray kaleidoscope of grief included sadness, anger, loneliness and guilt. Tears spilled out at inopportune times. Anger boiled over for no reason. Friends drifted.

Hospice sent reading materials monthly on dealing with grief. After all that had happened and all the social worker helped me with, the paper seemed worthless.

Scarlet O'Hara from *Gone with the Wind* must be one reason for society's callousness of grief. Her flippant refusal to wear black following the death of her unloved husband was surely to blame.

I wanted to wear black. I wanted someone to hear me, someone to care. American culture demanded I get over the loss and move on.

As I wrote a letter to the Hospice Company, my embittered feelings spilled onto the page. I felt abandoned by the social worker. A visit for a bereaved family member seemed much more appropriate than empty pamphlets.

The Hospice Company graciously gave me three sessions with a grief counselor. She heard my frustration with an uncaring society. She gently

BEFORE YOU DEPART

helped me realize my anger aimed at those who refused to hear me. They simply had no experience to compare with my loss.

They were uninformed, but probably not uncaring. They could not understand what being separated from those who had shaped my life was like. All of my life, my parents and other relatives had contributed to birthdays, Christmas and other special occasions.

Perhaps those individuals who had experienced loss did not have a close bond or a loving relationship. She suggested I hold on to what was good and let go of anything that was not.

One symbolic exercise included blowing up balloons. Each balloon represented the negatives contributing to anger and resentment. My bouquet of balloons full, I then popped each one and let go of what was no longer life-giving.

The counselor also felt that a grief support group would help. My excuses included the long drive to Tulsa. And legitimately that my children had long neglected needs. She understood, reinforcing the need to focus on what was good concerning my care for Dad and my relationship with him.

Slowly my focus shifted to new things. The Master Gardener Class required a project of giving back to the community. The nursing home Dad was in had an empty courtyard that needed new plants and landscaping. The children from the botany class and their parents joined me in a labor of love for the residents of the nursing home.

A local nursery donated plants and assisted in the landscape design. The class planted new growth in the flower beds and gave new life to the nursing home's outdoor patio. The children also baked cookies and passed them out to the residents. The activities director and nursing home staff loved our efforts.

Three months following Dad's death, Emma called. "Nanette, I need you to pray for me. I have to have a hysterectomy tomorrow."

"Sure, I'll pray for you. Let me know when it's over and how you're doing."

BEFORE YOU DEPART

With urgency and panic in her voice, she said, "No, I want you to pray now!"

"God, please be with Emma as she goes through surgery. Please guide the surgeon and perfect all that concerns her. Amen."

After the surgery Emma called. "Everything is fine. I just have to take it easy for a few days."

That following Monday, she called back with a new joy in her voice. "I was baptized yesterday and received Jesus into my heart."

"That's wonderful news." Another answer to prayer. I hung up the phone and praised God for His faithful answer to another prayer.

God continued to work in Emma's life. He remained silent in mine. Despite the quiet, I knew God remained faithful. Perhaps He was letting me rest after our long journey.

Family curses were being broken. Shame died with Dad.

But my grief continued. Insomnia met me each night. Exhausted, I went to the doctor who put me on an antidepressant. I finally slept. The frequent crying stopped. The side effects were weight gain. Fifty pounds in three months.

My grief eventually led me to Al-Anon, a support group for families who have a loved one suffering from the disease of alcoholism. Although my current situation did not include anyone who drank, the group fit my needs. They provided a safe place to grieve and express my feelings surrounding Dad's death.

After completion of the Master Gardener Course, I learned about a Grape Management Course. My interest piqued. The class spanned eight months. One class per month offered in Perkins, Oklahoma. I enrolled.

I enjoyed the class but learned that tending a vineyard was labor intensive. The responsibility of the vineyard would be primarily mine because of Andy's six-nights-a-week schedule.

At the conclusion of the class we visited vineyards south of Oklahoma City. One viticulturist was a single woman with a two-acre vineyard. If she could manage, maybe I could too. Certainly with help from Andy and the boys, I could execute the project.

The grape management class concluded, we prepared the two-and-a-half acre plot and ordered our grape vines. One thousand, six hundred vines of four different varieties of table grapes. Fruit for eating instead of wine making. Most other growers in the class had plans for wineries. My plan was to eventually invite people to come and pick grapes, to enjoy being outdoors with their families.

Spring came and so did planting time. The anxious euphoria of the new project waned as Andy and the boys used a post-hole digger to make sixty-five holes for just one row. Each hole was one-foot deep spaced evenly apart on the first 400-foot row. Twenty-five rows to go. We planted the starts that looked like sticks with a fibrous root system. The stick was then pruned to a two-inch twig. What I thought would take a week, took us two months.

The field full of grape potential would not produce for three or four years. But the vines still needed spraying, weeding, pruning, weed-eating, mowing and watering. The twigs of potential grew quickly. Each vine needed to be trained onto its own vertical cane. The first winter Andy and the boys erected the trellis system to support the mature vines. The pruning and training were my job.

All was on schedule until the second year of growth. Drought threatened to desecrate the vines. Watering each vine with a fifty-gallon tank of water behind the tractor did little to revive the wilted plants. The plan to put in an irrigation system as time permitted was now a crash project.

Notifying a local nursery of our predicament, they placed the vineyard on top of their priority list. The irrigation system was installed the following week providing life-giving water to the scorched vines.

Tending the vineyard was therapeutic to my aching heart. The grip of grief continued with inconvenient waves of sadness. The vineyard gave me a connection to Dad. The chores were familiar and dear, reminiscent of helping Dad in the peach and pear orchard.

BEFORE YOU DEPART

The vineyard was my part in keeping a family tradition of farming alive. The work was simple and satisfying, connecting me to the earth. I felt certain my purpose in life was tied to the vineyard and nurturing fruit production. A job appointed by God.

As the vines matured and began to bear fruit, I sold them at the Claremore Farmer's Market. Another familiar task that continued my connection with fruit production and sales.

My soap was a natural addition to sales at the farmer's market. I started a company named Oklahoma Rose Pure and Natural Soaps and named the grape production Oklahoma Rose Vineyard.

Further expansion of my enterprise led me to open a small café in the apartment where Dad had resided. When people came to pick grapes they could enjoy some coffee and gourmet sandwiches along with a decadent dessert.

My overly zealous ambition spread my time and talents too thin. The Renaissance woman within did not have the necessary income to keep the vineyard in production and the café open. The location for Oklahoma Rose Vineyard and Café was not on a major highway. Although everyone who stopped in loved the food, the business was not sustainable. My dream slipped away.

Dwindling finances forced me to reenter the workforce. My job hunt included the local newspaper. Maybe I could write. No luck.

My search continued in the classified ads. The opportunities were limited. One nursing job was listed. *Hospice nurse wanted.*

My list of excuses not to go back into nursing rose up. *High stress level. Hadn't worked in the field for several years. Did I really want to do that?*

God continued to be silent. But over the past months, my dreams had included old nursing jobs. I thought they were nightmares. Or was God trying to lead me in another direction? Certainly I had firsthand experience with end-of-life issues through both parents' deaths to cancer.

BEFORE YOU DEPART

Reluctantly my car headed for the Hospice address. The door was locked. Probably a fly-by-night operation.

As I walked back to the car, two ladies pulled up next to me. Smiling, the redhead asked, "Are you here about the registered nurse position?"

"Yes."

"We're just getting back from lunch. I'm glad we didn't miss you. Come on in and we'll talk."

"I haven't worked in a while. The last few years I've been homeschooling my children and taking care of my dad."

A few more questions and the job was mine.

My approach to patients and their families was a ministry. I felt honored to be included in their end-of-life journeys. My own experience lent itself to those God put in my care. My goal was to ensure that each patient had all needs met — spiritually, physically and mentally. My fervent prayer that God would impart to each family exactly what they needed before their loved one departed into eternity.

I was well-suited to the position. Still grieving for Dad, compassion and sensitivity was magnified to the unique needs of patient and family.

I was the on-call nurse. My responsibility was to take care of patients' needs after office hours. If a patient called with a change in condition or was nearing death, I provided bedside care, obtaining vital signs and assessing the condition. If the patient was near death, I stayed until he or she passed, providing support to the family.

One night I was called to a nursing home. A patient was nearing death. She had no family. Entering the room in prayer, my assessment revealed that she had Cheyne Stokes breathing. Her other vital signs, blood pressure and oxygen levels were normal. The closer a person gets to death, the blood pressure and oxygen levels trend down.

Her condition meant I would probably be with her most of the night and possibly into the next morning. She was unresponsive, but I held her hand and prayed for her. I reached for the Gideon Bible and read, "Precious in the sight of the Lord is the death of his saints" (Psalm 116:15 KJV). The patient died immediately.

Time and time again I witnessed God's intimate touch as individuals completed their journeys on earth and entered eternity. But after eight years, the loss of patients began to take a personal toll.

God led me into Hospice by opening and closing doors. His grace allowed me to care for those with terminal illness and eventual death. But His grace seemed to be diminishing.

Yearning for a change, my attention turned to higher education. I taught as an adjunct nursing instructor in different institutions.

Eventually I enrolled in Southern Nazarene University, obtaining a master's degree in Nursing Education. My capstone project was "Prolonged Grief Disorder in Caregivers."

Research taught me that approximately twenty percent of caregivers suffer from grief that extends well beyond the usual six months to one year.

Individuals often became sick during or after their caregiving experience, suffering from hypertension, cancer, cardiac disease, suicidal thoughts, major depression and even death. Caregivers require care themselves but often neglect to seek help due to the stress of caring for a loved one.

As Baby Boomers age and require care, their caregivers may find themselves in situations similar to mine.

The journey of my dad's final year on earth was carefully orchestrated by God's tender loving touch. God held each of us in His grasp. God completed every last detail and answered each of my prayers before Dad departed.

BEFORE YOU DEPART

INVITATION

You may be a caregiver. You do not have to traverse this journey alone. God is available to you for strength, patience, comfort or any other need.
His greatest desire is to have daily fellowship with you as you pray and ask God for what you need. He will always hear you. He loves you.
He loves you so much, He sent His son Jesus to die for you on a cruel cross. His blood was shed for you so that sin would no longer separate you from God.
Invite God into your life. Include God in each and every circumstance you are facing. God desires to care for each intimate detail of your life.
He knows what you need before you ask. Matthew 6:8 or Hebrews 4:16
Watch and see what God Almighty will do for you and your loved ones.
I am praying for you and your loved ones. Open your heart to God and let the journey begin.

BEFORE YOU DEPART

BEFORE YOU DEPART

ACKNOWLEDGEMENTS

To Steve, my husband and greatest fan. The man who patiently accepted and wholeheartedly supported this endeavor.

To Rebecca Thesman, my writing coach and editor, who helped me turn a dream into a reality and helped me each small step along this journey. Whose encouragement and guidance were invaluable.

For all the women of God who faithfully prayed for me during this journey: Denece Parsons, Willa Kerby, Anita Gebbard, Linda Stewart, Linda Polson, Carol Round, Nancy Bethea, Dr Anne GhostBear, Dr Barbara Hannah.

Thank you for your love, support and prayer.

BEFORE YOU DEPART

84

BEFORE YOU DEPART

ABOUT THE AUTHOR

Nanette M. Holloway was a caregiver to both her mother and father. Both died from cancer. Her difficult journey through the muddy swamp of caregiving led her to write this publication.

Nanette is a registered nurse currently working in home health. Prior career choices include Hospice, Adjunct Clinical Instructor, and Mother-baby care. She approaches nursing as a ministry, caring for the body, mind and spirit.

Nanette and her husband live in the Midwest on eighty acres. They have two grown sons who she homeschooled.

Gardening is a favorite past time. At various times she and her family cultivated a vineyard and large vegetable garden, taking the produce to the local farmer's market. She also raises flowers and has completed the Master Gardener course through Oklahoma State University.

Holloway enjoys speaking and addressing audiences struggling with caregiving issues.

BEFORE YOU DEPART

Nanette holds a bachelor's of science degree in nursing from Oral Roberts University and a master's degree in Nursing Education from Southern Nazarene University.

Nanette has also written *Coping Skills for Caregivers* available on amazon.com. This publication was written out of her own desperate needs during and after her caregiving journey. Self-neglect culminated in prolonged grief following her father's death. This book provides the reader with simple, practical suggestions for self-care during your journey of caregiving.

Follow her on Facebook and Linked In. Subscribe to her blog at: https://nanetteholloway.com. Connect with God in the beauty of the garden and follow her caregiving blogs.

Then post a review of *Before You Depart on* Amazon and Goodreads.

BEFORE YOU DEPART

OTHER BOOKS BY
NANETTE M. HOLLOWAY

Coping Skills for Caregivers